How 'l ⌐ Herd Cats;
Leading a team of independent thinkers.

By Simon Hartley

Printed by CreateSpace

"Brilliantly practical, this book makes you think, question and act. Another world class read.
Simple messages with clear calls to action to make your team better. Packed with lessons that you can implement today. A must for anyone wanting to improve their team."

Toby Babb, Managing Director, Harrington Starr.

"Fascinating book which provides a real insight into the structure, activity and performance of teams of all shapes and sizes. Some real easy take-aways that should be in the back of every leader's mind when trying to get the right results"

Steve Baker, Business Leader and Entrepreneur.

"There are very few business writers who seriously look to the future and address the issues that are coming round the corner. In How To Herd Cats, Simon Hartley has pulled together some very valuable concepts and lessons, from research and his own experiences, for those who are concerned about how to lead in a knowledge based economy. While the questions Simon poses may seem disconnected to the world we have grown up with in, the implications for the future of leadership are very profound. Don't measure this book by it thickness measure it by the light bulbs it turns on in your head".

Richard Bosworth, Chairman of The What If? Forums.

"In business, you're only as strong as your weakest link. So how do you marshal a group of individuals to make them all play for the same team and for the benefit of the group? Simon Hartley digs into is extensive expertise and genius thinking and comes up with some practical strategies for creating change. This book shows how to empower people to make decisions to further the benefit of everyone in the business and not just themselves. This is a must read for anyone in a leadership role and especially those in the legal profession!"

Elizabeth Ward, Principal, Virtuoso Legal

| Contents

| Acknowledgements

I would like to say a huge thank you to everyone that has helped make this book possible.

Firstly, thank you very much, Dr Dan Franks. His insights into world class animal teams have been fascinating and enlightening.

I would also like to thank Floyd Woodrow for writing the Foreword for this book, and sharing his valuable thoughts with us.

Thank you to all of those who have worked on this project, reviewed this book, given their honest feedback and their endorsements. I am very grateful for them all.

Finally, thank you for reading it. I hope that you gain as much value from these very simple concepts as I have.

I dedicate this book to my gorgeous wife and wonderful daughters.

For almost 20 years, I have had the pleasure of working with elite athletes and sports teams. Some of these athletes and teams are amongst the very best in the world; world champions, world record breakers, top five world-ranked players, Olympians, gold medallists, and championship winning teams. As a sport psychology consultant, my job is to help them get their mental game right. Put simply, I help them to hone their focus, control their confidence, master their motivation, de-construct pressure and love their 'discomfort zone'.

Around 10 years ago, I also started to apply this stuff that I called 'sport psychology' to other disciplines; business, education, healthcare and the charity sector. To my amazement, I found that the same strategies that helped athletes perform better also worked outside of sport. How strange, I thought. How did that work? And then it dawned on me. I had been under the impression that I'd been applying sport psychology in business. The reality is that I was applying human performance psychology to sport all along, and I had simply begun to apply the same approaches to other fields.

This very simple shift in thinking has made a big impact on me. It kick-started my curiosity. I have always been fascinated to understand what differentiates world class athletes. What sets the champions apart from the rest? Now my intrigue has grown. I'm also curious to know what differentiates world class performers in vastly different disciplines. What common characteristics do they all share? What about world class leaders, teams and organisations? These questions have inspired me to study the very best leaders and teams in the world. In answering these questions, I've uncovered some powerful insights about leaders and the way they enable their teams to perform at their peak. Some leaders face a greater challenge; to galvanise a team of independent thinkers. So, how can a study of the world's greatest teams help us to lead our team? I would like to share some of my findings and insights with you in this short book. These simple, yet profound, principles can help us all to become more effective leaders, to galvanise our teams and enable them to deliver great performances consistently.

I hope you gain as much benefit as I have from these very simple ideas.

| Foreword, by Floyd Woodrow, MBE.

Simon is a game changer who wants to give individuals and teams tools to improve their performance and raise their game to the highest levels. I have had the pleasure of getting to know Simon over the last few years and I am not surprised that he has written another excellent book to compliment his work to date. His use of story-telling is excellent and I love the way he has drawn analogies to the animal kingdom in understanding performance. As I often say "nature is very unfair to those that do not evolve". I have no hesitation in commending this book to you.

Floyd M Woodrow MBE DCM

For more information on Floyd Woodrow, visit
http://www.chrysalis-worldwide.com/associates/
floydwoodrow
Twitter: @floydwoodrow

The purpose of this book is very simple. It exists to help you to herd your human 'cats'. I'm sure that you'll recognise the challenge of engaging a collection of independent thinkers, with their own ideas, egos, agendas and self-interests. How do we galvanise such people into an effective team? How do we align them and ensure that everyone is on the same page and pulling in the same direction?

Whilst working with and studying the very best teams in the world, I have noticed that there are some very simple, practical and powerful approaches that we can all employ. These are not rocket science and I suspect they're not unique to this book either; you may even have come across a few of them before. There is a temptation that we could overlook these simple principles because we've seen them or heard them before. We often have a habit of thinking, "I know all that; move on". As you read this book, you might find it beneficial to ask some questions if you notice these kinds of thoughts beginning to surface in your mind. Instead of thinking, "Yes, I've heard it before", what would happen if you asked...?

"So, how well do we actually do this at the moment?"
"How could we improve?"
"Do we do these things consistently well?"

This is not 'War and Peace'. It won't take you long to read from cover to cover. This is not a big book, and it doesn't have to be. The ideas are very simple. However, it can take a while for you to really understand the impact that these ideas can have on your leadership and the performance of your team. I've included some case studies and examples of how other people have applied these simple concepts to phenomenal effect. Although we can often pick up helpful tips from reading other people's experiences, it is far more important that you can adopt the principles in your own life.

My hope is that, by reading this book, you can begin to bring your team together and realise their true potential.

Why Learn From World Class Teams?

I employ a very straight forward rationale. I invest time studying a wide range of teams and leaders at the very pinnacle of their field. I'm interested in identifying the common characteristics that they all share. My theory is that common traits, which are displayed in very diverse disciplines, are likely to be pretty generic. If that's the case, then it stands to reason that when we begin to adopt those characteristics ourselves, we too could become great.

In an increasingly demanding world, being average means being vulnerable. Size is no guarantee of success or even survival these days. Becoming ever better has become a necessity, not a luxury. I don't believe that constant improvement helps you win the game anymore, it just keeps you in the game. The stark reality is that if we're not moving forwards quicker than our competition, we're going backwards. Therefore, finding a competitive advantage has become crucial to both survival and success.

I recently spoke at an event, called Leadership In The 21st Century. There were an array of exceptional leaders from business, sport, the military and extreme expeditions. As I listened to them speak, I heard them outlining the challenges that their teams had faced. How do you bring together a team of volunteer 'Games-makers' to host the London 2012 Olympic Games? How do you enable a team of people, who have never stepped onto an ice-cap, to reach the North Pole unsupported? How do you create teams capable of winning Olympic gold medals or completing combat missions against all the odds? Although their challenges seemed different on the face of it, there was an underlying theme. Each of the teams encountered the unknown. Their fundamental challenge was navigating the unpredictable situations and events that unfolded. This is a common challenge for most leaders and emphasises the importance of having a great team. Challenges are guaranteed. Uncertainty is a given. It reminded me of a conversation that I had with a former SAS Major.

"We don't know what the challenges will be, but we know that together we're equipped to deal with them".

What Can We Learn From World Class Teams?

World class teams are, by definition, elite. They are made up of high performing individuals. The SAS recruit the very best soldiers from the British Army. When the Red Arrows select their team, they pick from the very best pilots in the Royal Air Force. Championship winning sports teams also contain elite athletes and players. Great sports teams often recruit players because of their creativity and individual flair. Former SAS Major, Floyd Woodrow, has worked with a wide variety of teams in both sport and business. Interestingly he described the SAS as the most entrepreneurial organisation that he's ever come across. SAS units need to be highly adaptable and are therefore composed of creative thinkers. Elite performers, by their very nature, are often the "cats" that we're looking to herd. They are independent thinkers.

Many sports coaches and managers understand that the elite players often come with the biggest egos. These players can be the toughest to manage. Their individuality makes them a great athlete, but can also create challenges when trying to galvanise the team.

There is no doubt that studying elite human teams can help us to herd our cats. However, they're not the only teams that we can learn from. Recently I have been studying some of the greatest teams from the animal kingdom to find out what makes them exceptional.

What Can We Learn From Animal Teams?

What can we learn from orca pods, flocks of pigeons and starlings or shoals of fish, which will help us lead our team? When I watch animal teams at work, I am often amazed by their incredible co-ordination. Have you ever seen the common bottlenose dolphins of Florida catching fish in the shallows? These clever mammals have adapted to their environment and developed a unique method of catching fish in the shallow water. By circling a shoal of fish while beating their tails against the silty bottom, the dolphins trap their prey in a ring of mud. The panicked fish jump out of the water away from the ring and straight into the waiting mouths of their fellow dolphins (BBC, 2009). It is an ingenious method that requires a great deal of team work.

You may also have seen orca pods creating bow waves that wash Weddell seals off of their protective ice floe. It is a spectacle that was first filmed by the BBC's Frozen Planet series in 2009 (BBC, 2011). It is only by coordinating their efforts that the whales can create a wave large enough to dislodge the seal and knock them into the water. But it is not only the more intelligent mammalian species that can produce spectacular examples of coordination. Flocks of starlings and shoals of fish display mesmerising synchronicity to avoid their predators.

Wonderful as these examples are, I'd argue that the real value we can gain from animal teams lays elsewhere. Animal teams show us the base principles of leadership and teamwork in action. Studying animal teams allows us to see teams operate without the baggage that humans tend to bring. We can see them in a pure form, stripped of the complications that seem to accompany human teams. In fact, I would argue that in many cases the animal teams are far more effective than human teams and there are plenty of lessons that we can learn from them.

Leaders face an array of challenges. Most teams have targets. In business, these could be KPI (Key Performance Indicator) driven targets, sales targets, profit targets or the demand to hit budget. In education, the targets could relate to student progression or performance. In sports, the targets normally relate to league position, win-loss records, trophies or medals. The challenge for the leader is often that they cannot directly deliver the team's target all by themselves. In addition, the targets are often outcomes and results rather than processes, which normally means that we have relatively little control over them anyway. Just how much control do we have over our ability to hit the sales target? Do we have complete control over the client's decision to buy? What about student progression in education? How much control does a teacher actually have over what the students learn? Interestingly, Robert Duke, a professor of music and human learning, delivered a keynote in 2008 entitled, "Why Students Don't Learn What We Think We Teach Them". It is an interesting thought because it challenges a very commonly held assumption. We might assume that learners learn what teachers and coaches are trying to teach them. It supposes that teachers and coaches, in some way, set the agenda. We assume that learning is led by the teacher and followed by the student. However, the reality is that the student will only ever learn when they are engaged, and they choose when to engage.

In reality, the leader only ever has indirect control over the team's performance and the likelihood that it will deliver the target.

Added to this, the leader is responsible for pulling their team together as a unit. In some cases the leader has the ability to recruit and select their team. However, that isn't always the case. Many leaders will inherit at least some of their team members. Even if the leader chooses the team members, it is very rare that they will choose each other. As such, there is a very real chance that the team members may not see eye-to-eye with the leader, or each other. As we have already discovered, there is also the inevitable challenge that is presented when we navigate the unknown. Whilst the leader may be happy to do this, there is no guarantee that the team will be as keen. The personality of many leaders tends to lend itself to taking on challenges, problem solving, finding creative solutions and navigating change. However, it is likely that at least some of the team may not be as comfortable with these demands.

And this is not an exhaustive list by any means.

To magnify these challenges, they don't come in isolation. When we combine these, we begin to see the demands that leaders tend to face on a daily basis. Most leaders are asked to ensure that their team delivers a result, which is outside of their control... with a collection of individuals they may not have chosen (and who haven't chosen each other)... with people who may not like change... in an environment that's constantly changing and increasingly uncertain.

Does any of that sound familiar?

Independent Thinkers & Competing Opinions.

The problem with human beings is that they have minds of their own. Sometimes they even remember that they have the ability to think for themselves. Ironically, independent thinkers can simultaneously be a leader's greatest challenge and greatest asset. The issues tend to arise, of course, when there is a difference of opinion between the leader and the team members. The strategy that the leader has formed may not match the opinions, wants or desires of the team.

Sometimes the team simply may not agree that the leader's solution is the best for the team. However, sometimes there are other dimensions as well. Is it possible that the team member knows that the plan being proposed is the right one, but it doesn't serve their individual interests?

CASE STUDY

I spoke recently to the Managing Partner of a Law Firm. Changes in regulations and market conditions have created a number of significant challenges to legal practices in the UK. Many firms are looking to change their structures, which inevitably threatens the status quo. In the past, the Equity Partners have typically enjoyed a generous remuneration package that also provides them with a healthy retirement package when they exit. Through my discussion with the Managing Partner, it became obvious that the senior members of the firm were becoming increasingly resistant to the proposed changes, even though they were clearly in the long term interests of the business. The source of this resistance was self-interest. There was a misalignment between the best interests of the firm and those of the Equity Partners. The strategy that best served the business actually threatened the positions, wealth and future prosperity of the partners.

Clearly, independent thinkers don't just bring competing opinions, but also competing agendas. Typically, human beings don't like change. However, when change appears to be less beneficial, it's unsurprising that we tend to resist it.

Do you recognise this dialogue?

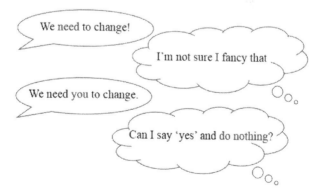

Competing Agendas & Egos.

Added to this, there is also the distinct possibility that our egos may also come into play. Leaders can find themselves embroiled in power struggles with team members who think that their way is best. It's quite possible that the team member has aspirations to become a leader and wants to flex their intellectual muscles. I have seen plenty of boardroom discussions that seem to revolve solely around one thing; the need to win the argument. Ridiculous as it seems, some discussions seem to have very little to do with finding the best solution to the problem. Instead, it appears that the aim is to dominate, to win or to be recognised by the others in the room.

What's actually most important? Is it finding the best solution for the team, or winning the argument? Is it point scoring? Is it looking good or positioning yourself within the business? Is the primary aim to build a career pathway by impressing others? Is it to create social currency and win the office politics game?

Is this familiar?

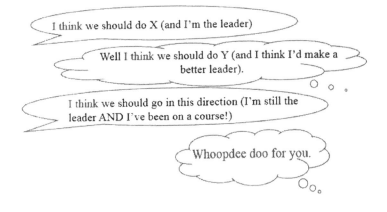

CASE STUDY

My P&L vs Your P&L.

Whilst working with a global corporation, I had a conversation with a senior manager. He was becoming increasingly frustrated that his team seemed to be battling against each other rather than working with each other. As we discussed this issue in more depth it became apparent that each of them had a P&L Target (Profit & Loss Target) to deliver for their part of the business. In simple terms, they each needed to ensure that their section delivered a specified level of profit; i.e. they made a certain amount of income and controlled the expenses. As we looked at how they generated their income and controlled the expenses, it also emerged that their individual agendas were actually in competition. They actually made decisions that enhanced their own P&L at the expense of someone else's. In order to deliver their own target, they actually competed directly against others and ultimately made it less likely that the team overall met its targets.

It is an interesting challenge for a leader. How can we get a team to pull together and deliver a collective performance if we have competing agendas?

CASE STUDY

"If only one of us can be successful around here, it's going to be me".

It may not surprise you to know that in elite professional team sports, competition for places can be brutal. Players in the English Premier League know that there is a huge financial difference between being a regular first team player and a fringe player or reserve team player. In addition to the financial difference, there is also a gulf in the level of fame and recognition that players receive. It therefore stands to reason that established players may react if they feel that their place in the first team is under threat from a young talented junior. I have seen senior players making the lives of those emerging players very difficult, in an attempt to inhibit their performance. From one perspective it seems crazy to deliberately reduce the performance of a teammate, who might help your team to become more successful. But, as we know, self-preservation is a powerful motive.

This pattern is not uncommon in business settings. There are often distinct differences between the motives and agendas of individuals and those of the team. In my work I have also found a misalignment between the priorities of individuals and that of the team. In many cases the individuals are inadvertently detracting from each other's performance, and therefore the team performance, in pursuit of their own targets.

CASE STUDIES

My KPI vs Your KPI

I have recently worked with a business that has an interesting, but not unique, challenge. The challenge, very simply, is that when individuals deliver their KPIs they actually disrupt others within the business. This particular example comes from a Recruitment Consultancy. In this company the recruitment consultants are targeted primarily on their fees and their business development. In the consultants view, anything that does not contribute directly towards those targets, such as admin, is a distraction. Unfortunately, the operations team and the management team in the company need the admin to be done so that they have accurate and timely information on which to base business critical decisions. By focusing on KPIs ahead of admin, the consultants give themselves a better chance of hitting their targets. However, they also inhibit the performance of the people around them and ultimately the whole business. Ah, it seems we have a problem.

Office Politics.

Are office politics a necessary evil for anyone that wants to succeed in corporate life? Are they a symptom of a poisonous environment? Or, are they simply an illustration of the way human beings operate in society? Is there really any difference between office politics and social climbers? However we might describe office politics, the one thing that most people agree upon is that they tend to detract from performance, and rarely (if ever) enhance it.

The reasons that people engage in office politics are fairly obvious. Often it is simply a way of trying to gain an advantage. In many cases people are looking for some form of personal advantage, but it could also be to advance a cause. When people engage in political manoeuvring, it is likely to be driven by a simple motive; "I want to be....". Some people might want to become the CEO, others might want to be better paid, better rewarded or more recognised. Often other people have the control over whether we become what we want, or not. Who makes the decision on promotions, pay increases, bonuses and awards? Who do I need to garner favour from? Who do I need to influence? How do I get them to form a positive opinion of me? In answering these questions, and trying to solve this problem, people might also look for ways to take credit for things that have gone well and deflect blame for things that didn't.

In my view, the presence of office politics simply illustrates that there are competing agendas at work. They show that we have some fundamental differences between the aims and interests of the members, and those of the team. In an environment where politics are rife, leaders see a group of people desperately trying to clamber over each other to reach the top. It is hardly the makings of a coherent team. Instead of a team pulling in the same direction, we see a collection of 'cats' all following their own self-interests and agendas.

Over To You.

How does all of this relate to you and your team?

What are your key leadership challenges?

Do you see competing opinions?

Do you see competing agenda?

Do you see people following their own self-interests ahead of those of the team?

Do you see people engaging in political manoeuvring, in an attempt to get where they want to be?

How about your own interests and agendas as a leader?

Do these compete with the team or the organisation?

Is there complete alignment, or a misalignment somewhere?

As we address these issues, you may find it useful to reflect back on how to apply them to your own challenges.

It's not a trick question. There are obviously some very good reasons why sheep choose to flock together. Fundamentally, they are prey animals, not predators. The reasons that they choose to flock together essentially hinge around the need to survive. A flock of 100 sheep have 100 pairs of eyes. The advantage to each sheep is that the group is more likely to spot a predator than any one individual sheep. It also means that whilst some members of the flock are watching, others can eat, and visa versa. Collectively this means that everyone gets to eat knowing that others are doing the watching. Being in a flock of 100 also means there are is, statistically, a reduced likelihood that you'll be the one that gets eaten. In a flock of 100, you have a 1% chance of being taken by a predator. In a flock of one your odds are not quite as good. Animals also tend to know that predators find it more difficult to target single members in large groups. The visual challenge is greater when there are lots of individuals moving en masse, meaning that bigger numbers become confusing to the predator.

This basic logic also applies to flocks of geese migrating many thousands of miles. No doubt you'll have seen the classic 'V shaped' formations that they adopt. There are of course a number of very good reasons why the geese choose to migrate together. Flying in a V shape is aerodynamically efficient for the flock as a whole, which means that each individual expends less energy than they would flying alone. In addition, each season there are young birds that have never made the journey before. Flying in a flock allows them to join the experienced navigators and also learn the route.

Why do Orca (Killer Whales) live in family groups, or pods? In the opening pages we discovered that together they are able to hunt prey that an individual alone would not be able to catch. Washing Weddell seals off of ice floes is one such example. Pods of fish-hunting Orca in the North Atlantic will often corral fish using a net of air bubbles, which some of the whales release from their blow holes. The fish will not swim through the bubbles so become trapped within them. With the fish confined, the remaining members of the pod stun the fish with their tails and create a bounty for all to share. Of course, the benefits of operating as a family unit don't stop there. Some pods don't hunt in unison, they do so individually. Even in these cases, the hunting territories and methods have often been handed down from generation to generation. Just like herds of elephants, the Orca families are led by a matriarch. In some cases she may be as much as three times as old as the oldest male. Unusually within the animal kingdom, the matriarchal females experience a menopause, meaning that they live long past the point at which they can reproduce. It is thought that the reasons for this center around their ability to pass on their expertise to future generations (Foster, et al, 2012).

Whichever animal teams we look at, there is one fundamental common thread. There is a very good reason why those individuals choose to operate together.

Very simply, it is in their best interests!

It is such a simple principle and therefore is easily overlooked. But it's incredibly important! In fact, it is so important that I'm going to say it again (in capitals).

IT IS IN THEIR INDIVIDUAL INTERESTS TO BE A PART OF THE TEAM.

The 'Why' Of The Team.

These animal teams illustrate a very simple but profound principle. There needs to be a strong and compelling reason for the team to exist, and for individuals to elect to be a part of it. This principle applies equally to human teams. If you look at many highly successful teams, you may start to see this at work. Take a sports team for example. Many of the players within the team realise that in order to be successful, they need the team to perform at its peak. Most players like winning; they aspire to become champions and win trophies. It is rare, although not impossible, that great individual performances alone can lead to long term success in team sports. More often, it is the team's performance that dictates success. The same is often true of rock bands. Although some musicians might split from the group to forge a solo career, many members of a band understand that their personal success is integrally linked to that of the group. It's tough to become a world renowned drummer if you haven't got a great band.

Author James Kerr, who studied the culture of the All Blacks, noted that they are guided by the understanding that "the strength of the wolf is in the pack" (Kerr, 2013)

Having a strong rationale for the team doesn't necessarily mean that all of the members will appreciate it. In his book, Sacred Hoops, Chicago Bulls basketball coach Phil Jackson (1995), describes the challenge of getting players to play for the team rather than showcasing their individual skills. He recognised that many NBA players saw fame and fortune following those 'superstars' that displayed the greatest individual flair on court. Phil Jackson's challenge at the Bulls was to help Michael Jordon, who was arguably the greatest individual player in history, to understand the benefits of playing for the team rather than just in the team. When Michael Jordan focused on helping the team perform at its best, their collective success was unprecedented. Interestingly, the success that the Bulls subsequently enjoyed as an organisation may also have helped Jordan himself to attain his 'legendary' status as player.

Some human teams have an even more powerful reason to commit to the team. SAS units, for example, depend upon each other for their very survival. The members of the team are utterly dependent upon each other as individuals and in the performance of the team. But, of course, it is not only their lives that are at stake often. The success of the SAS unit in a combat situation, often impacts upon the lives of many other soldiers and civilians.

There needs to be a strong reason why members will opt to belong to a team. This simple base principle is often fundamental to the success of the team.

Asking The Stupid Questions

Everyone has their own specialist skills. One of mine is to ask stupid questions. Last year I spoke at an event for around 300 business leaders in the City of London. These particular executives all operated in the finance, technology and commodities sectors. One of the delegates at the event, who was a senior banker, asked me a pretty straight forward question...

"How do I get my team of traders to work as a team?"

I answered him with a stupid question.

"Why do they need to operate as a team?"

His answer was probably shared by many other business leaders around the globe. He said...

"Because they are my team and I am their leader, so I need them to work together".

Unfortunately, that's not a particularly compelling reason to work together. To delve a little deeper I then asked,

"What benefit will the traders get from working together? Will they do more trading, deliver better results or make life easier for each other?"

The business leader's answer...

"I'm not sure".

Let's take a moment to look at some of the teams that operate in business, education, healthcare, charities and even the military. Some of those teams obviously do have a strong raison d'etre. In medicine, surgical teams can collectively accomplish things that even the greatest surgeon alive could not hope to achieve alone. However, there are other examples where the rationale for the team may not be so clear.

Does a sales team really need to operate as a team? Do the sales executives actually gain benefit from working together, or would they be better off ploughing a lone furrow? How much time and effort is required to work together and pass information between themselves? How much benefit will they actually gain from doing it? The sales manager may argue that they would benefit from sharing leads, for example. But, do the sales executives actually want to share their leads, or would they rather keep hold of the leads they have and focus on using them to deliver their own targets?

These examples show that the presence of a strong reason on its own may not be enough. In order to get the members of a team to choose to work together, they have to understand and appreciate those reasons. They have to see that there is a vested interest in being part of that team because it serves them. Put simply, they need to know why investing themselves into the team is a "no brainer".

Do We Create Teams In Name Only?

Are we really a team, or are we simply a collection of job titles?

Are we really a team, or do we just share the same brand... or wear the same shirt?

Many of the 'teams' that I've seen don't operate as teams. For example, does the Board of a company actually work as a team, or are they just together because their job title contains the word 'Director'. When I walk into boardrooms to work with companies, I often find the same job titles present; Managing Director, Finance Director, Sales Director, Operations Director, HR Director, etc. These people come together for board meetings, on predetermined occasions, with a pre-specified agenda. More often than not, they'll deliver their reports, ask a few questions, agree some actions, shake hands and then leave. Is that really a team at work? Do we simply refer to a collection of sales executives as "a sales team" because it's conventional, or because they actually operate as a team? Are they actively delivering a performance or executing a mission together? Are they harnessing their collective power and resources to solve a problem?

Recently I have been working with the Equity Partners (EPs) of a leading Commercial Law Firm in the UK. Each of the EPs heads up an area of the business, such as Commercial Law, Employment Law, Property Law, and so on. On several occasions I have heard the EPs referring to their own 'practice', within the overall Firm (i.e. the 'property practice' or 'employment law practice'). Traditionally, it seems, they have operated as teams within these 'practices', but not collaborated as a united team across the Firm. I asked the EPs...

"Is this really a team, or do you simply share a brand?"

It is a similar question to one that I asked a professional sports team.

"Is this really a team or do you just wear the same shirts?"

So, what's the difference between a team, and a collection of job titles? Does your team actually operate as a team, or is that just the name you give it?

Over To You

What is the compelling reason for your team to work together?

How does it serve the interests of each individual?

Do the members understand and appreciate the value of the team, and why there is a vested interested in committing to it?

Is it a "no brainer"?

What's your reason for being part of the team?

Do the players in your team play for the team, or just in the team?

Do you play for the team, or in the team?

There is a great reason why sheep flock together, Orca form pods and geese fly in a V formation. Of course, the same does not apply to cats (with the exception perhaps of lions). Of course the reason for this is simple. There is no good rationale for cats to live together or hunt together. In fact, it may even be more advantageous for cats to operate alone. Their modus operandi is based on stalking prey. So, if we want our people to operate as a team, why would we recruit 'cats'? Surely it would make more sense to employ sheep, right?

The Value of Independent Thinkers.

Earlier in this book we reflected that independent thinkers might be the leader's greatest challenge, but they are also potentially their greatest asset. In fact, most organisations deliberately recruit people because of their ability to think for themselves. How many times have you heard leaders and managers say, "I need people who will use their own initiative" and, "We want people to innovate". Those are not qualities that you find in 'sheep'. No doubt, you'll also have seen job adverts that say, "We want bright people that will think for themselves; self-starters with entrepreneurial flair". Many organisations deliberately look to balance internal recruitment with external, so that they bring in "fresh thinking". The aim of all of this, obviously, is to ensure that we have people who can provide creative solutions. In an uncertain environment, this ability is vital. Remember...

"We don't know what the challenges will be, but we know that together we're equipped to deal with them". SAS Major, Floyd Woodrow.

The Waikato Chiefs, from New Zealand, won back-to-back Super Rugby Championships in 2012 and 2013. Unusually, in rugby union, they often didn't dominate the possession or territory statistics. In spite of this, they out-scored their competition because their opponents found it very difficult to defend against them. The reason for this is relatively straight forwards; they were unpredictable. This didn't happen by chance, or because they had supremely talented players. It resulted because the Chief's coaching team gave the players license to try things, to do things differently, to experiment, find creative solutions on the field of play; to use their power of independent thought.

However, the value of independent thought extends beyond having individuals capable of providing some creative solutions. In fact, there is a body of evidence which suggests that even the most talented and expert individuals will never be as wise as a collective.

The Wisdom Of Crowds.

In 1906 Francis Galton, a British scientist, conducted an experiment to show that experts were more intelligent than a crowd of non-experts. To prove his hypothesis, he attended the West of England Fat Stock and Poultry Exhibition near his home in Plymouth. During the exhibition there was a competition, to estimate the weight of an ox. The beast was placed on display and the members of the crowd placed a wager on how much the ox would weigh once it had been slaughtered, butchered and dressed. Galton expected the estimates of the experts (farmers and butchers) to be significantly closer than that of the non-expert crowd. Upon analysing all of the entries Galton discovered, to his amazement, that when he took an average of all of the crowd's estimates it came in at 1,197 pounds. The actual slaughtered, dressed weight of the ox was 1,198 pounds. Incredibly, the non-expert crowd were far more accurate than the most accurate individual 'expert' amongst them (Surowiecki, 2004).

Author and journalist, James Surowiecki, expands on Galton's findings. Of course, what Francis Galton discovered extends beyond estimating the weight of cattle. Surowiecki provides an array of other examples across many different disciplines, including Google and the stock-market. He suggests that given the right conditions, the team's collective solution is better than that of any one individual.

In order to be wise, a group decision needs to be the aggregation of diverse, independent, thoughts. This means that, as Galton's crowd did at the agricultural show, each individual presents their own independent thoughts. These independent thoughts are then aggregated. The crowd did not get together and discuss the weight of the ox and then submit a collective estimate. In many group discussions it will be the voices of the most dominant members that are heard, not the voice of the group. Inevitably, there will be input from the less dominant members that never gets included and therefore cannot impact upon the final conclusion. Even the order in which people speak has an effect on the course of the discussion. In fact, human beings have been shown not to publically contradict a group, even if it means going against their own convictions. Therefore, if the group were to discuss the weight of the ox, the conclusion would not represent the input of the crowd as a whole.

As well as independent thoughts, the crowd requires diversity of thought. In Galton's case, the crowd was made up of almost 800 different people with their own backgrounds, levels of knowledge and experience. Each of them had their own personal input. Both of these elements are critical in allowing us to discover the collective wisdom in our teams.

Lack Of Independent Thought.

For teams to operate successfully, there undoubtedly needs to be a degree of togetherness. It's highly unlikely that a team will be successful if everyone operates completely independently from each other. However, togetherness on its own may not lead to success either. Let's take our sheep as an example. As we have discussed, they are a flocking animal. Therefore, they are driven to stick together. In fact, when they perceive danger, this tendency is exacerbated. It would be safe to bet that they'll always run together. The question is, where will they run? In truth, sheep often run exactly where the shepherd and sheep dog want them to run. Sometimes this is into the back of a truck that drives them to the abattoir. The point is that being in the wrong place, together, is not necessarily the outcome that we're looking for.

William Beebe, an American naturalist, witnessed an unusual phenomenon in the jungles of Guyana. He observed a group of army ants, marching in a circle measuring 1,200 feet in circumference. The loop took each ant two and a half hours to complete. Perhaps more astonishingly, the ants marched in this circle for two days until most of them dropped dead. It is a phenomenon known as a 'circular mill' (Surowiecki, 2004).

Ant colonies are highly successful and normally operate extremely well. There are some very simple rules that allow them to function. These rules govern each ant's behavior. One such rule says that, when lost, you simply follow the ant in front of you. This ensures that the ants remain together, which is essential for them to thrive and survive. It also works well when they're on a predetermined path. Ants often navigate routes by using pheromones and scents, which can become interrupted by the environment. Unfortunately, if one or two ants stray from the predetermined route for some reason, the system fails because no ant is capable of independent thought. Ants are programmed to obey the very simple rules that allow their colony to function, so no-one breaks the cycle of death. It seems that their greatest strength can also be their greatest weakness.

Independent Thought & Critical Input.

With independent thinking comes the potential for critical input. If we want our people to think for themselves, there is a good chance that they will not think the same way that we do. Rather than endorsing our plan, they may question it, challenge it or even find some dirty great holes in it. If we recruited them because we actively want bright people who will use their own initiative, this has got to be a good thing... right?

I suspect that the challenge comes when this critical feedback actually impacts on the leader's ego. If we've come up with the plan, we might also want it to be a good plan. We might like it when people to say lovely things like, "That's a great plan boss" because it makes us feel good. Conversely, if one of our team turns around as says, "I don't think much of that plan", it might well have the opposite effect. Perhaps one of the greatest challenges that a leader of independent thinkers faces, is to accept critical input from the team. Many leaders are more senior than the team members that they lead. Taking critical input from junior members can be tough. As a senior person, we may also be more knowledgeable and experienced. However, it doesn't necessarily mean that we'll have the best answer. Unfortunately, it could mean that we think we have the best answer. As the science behind the wisdom of crowds suggests, even the greatest individual expert is unlikely to create a solution to rival that of the group.

Leaders who opt to protect their decision, opinion or position, tend to create conflict with the independent thinkers who challenge them. In doing so, they're likely to alienate themselves from the team, rather than engage with it. And so the dialogue begins...

"I think we should do X (and I'm the leader)"

"I think we should do Y (and I think I'd make a better leader)".

Of course, those who opt to use the critical input may end up with a better plan.

Over To You.

Do you recruit cats, and then wish they were sheep?

Do you encourage your cats to become sheep?

Do you adopt the approach taken by the coaches at the Waikato Chiefs, and give your team the license to be unpredictable?

Do you actively draw on the wisdom of your 'crowd'?

Do you seek critical input from your independent thinkers and invite them to enhance your plan?

Have you ever watched a shoal of sardines moving almost 'as one' to avoid a predator? They display an astonishing level of synchronicity. As the marlin dives towards the shoal, the mass of fish seem to create a void around their enemy and then seamlessly reform. It continually breaks and reforms, eluding the marlin. Looking at the shoal, it is tempting to view them as an amazing team. They seem to be governed by one mind. To the onlooker, it appears that they collectively decide how and where they move. However, the truth is that they don't operate as a team at all. The sardines don't collectively decide to move in any given direction. Instead, they independently decide to do the same thing. Like flocks of starlings, the sardines actually function according to a few simple principles. One is to stay as close to the middle of the shoal as possible. Another is to get out the way of the predator. If the predatory marlin approached from the right, it's likely that the sardines would all individually opt to move to the left in order to escape. They also seek to be in the centre, which results in the shoal continually reforming. The reality is that each sardine makes an independent decision that is based on its own self-interest. Interestingly, this gives the impression that they're making a group decision.

We can see the same kinds of mass independent decision making in humans. Our decisions to purchase the same product might appear to be collective, but in reality are independent. The discipline of economics tries to predict buying trends by assuming that each individual will act in their own self-interest. There are other obvious examples such as political voting in parliamentary or presidential elections. Our use of language often suggests that we think collectively. Phrases like "the public decided", give the impression that there is a group consensus. Of course, the truth is that we vote independently, based on our own personal views and often with our own self-interest at heart.

A Common Response

The shoal of sardines also shows that collections of individuals can elicit a common response to changes in their environment. This principle works in both the animal kingdom and in humans. In its most elementary form, ants use environmental information to shape the way they respond. Rather than making decisions, they simply use the same set of rules to govern individual response. If X happens, I do Y. When all of the ants operate by the same rules, the change in X leads every individual to do Y.

Interestingly, some of the greatest human teams also use these principles to ensure that they work effectively as a team. My studies into elite racing yacht crews reveals that they have similar challenges. The crews need to constantly respond to changes in wind, water conditions and the opposing boats. To ensure that they respond as a team, each of the sailors has a clear idea of how the crew will respond to a given situation, and their individual role. If everyone detects the change in the wind direction, and knows what to do, the crew will respond without the need to make a group decision in the moment. I have found that this approach is also integral to the operation of SAS units in combat and a Formula One (F1) pit crew. In some situations the team just doesn't have the luxury to discuss changes. In Formula One, a pit stop to change all four wheels on the car will last approximately 2.5 seconds from start to finish. There is simply not enough time to issue a command, never mind have a discussion.

The Importance Of Understanding Self-Interest.

Our ability to herd cats actually hinges on our ability to embrace independent decision making. It may seem paradoxical at first, but independent decisions are not necessarily different. People, and animals, often decide to do exactly the same thing. Added to this, we can make our own decisions, following our own self-interests, and still opt to do the same thing. As the examples show, just because we make independent choices, doesn't necessarily mean that we'll choose to go in different directions.

Let's also remember that sometimes people elect to belong to teams and to act together. Sometimes being together is in the self-interests of each individual. As we have discussed, some teams have a compelling reason to exist. As such, the members choose to invest themselves in it. Situations often dictate that people will opt to join the team, rather than go it alone. Adversity has often been thought of as a force that galvanises a team.

Herding Our Cats

So, how does all this help us to herd our cats?

Accepting that independent thinking can lead people to work together, and even decide the same things, gives us a starting point. In fact, it may also stimulate a few questions.

"What are my cats likely to independently choose?"

"Which options would serve their individual self-interests?"

"Which direction are they most likely to opt for?"

"Are they likely to choose to invest in the team, because it serves them?"

Of course, to answer these questions, we have to know our people! We need to understand what motives them and the basis on which they're likely to make decisions.

CASE STUDY

The Misunderstood Sales Manager

It is human nature to pigeon-hole people and make assumptions as to what motivates them. One such assumption is that Sales Managers are motivated by targets and bonuses. Whilst that may be true, I think it's important to look at what's beyond the target. What's important to this person? If they say it is the money, what will that money buy?

In this case, our misunderstood sales manager was given an annual sales target. If he met the target at the end of the year, he would earn a promotion and join the board as the Sales Director. After a great deal of hard work, the sales manager hit the target. The Managing Director assumed that he'd be delighted when he received the news of his promotion, position on the board and job title. Interestingly, the promotion didn't come with a pay rise.

When I spoke to the Sales Director, he told me that he'd worked for the target to secure a pay rise. He has a disabled son and needed the money to build an extension to his house, which they would turn into a sensory room for him. The reason that he'd put in the extra hours to hit his target, was driven by his desire to provide for his family and take care of his young son. That's what really motivated him to hit the target.

I was asked the following question, by a senior leadership team.

"How can we better understand our team? What questions should we ask them?"

In my view, there are some base principles that might help.
- Spend time.
- Give people permission to be themselves and then observe them.
- Ensure that you create a 'judgment free' environment.
- Let them talk about themselves, their views, opinions, desires and thoughts.
- Listen. Be interested. Care.

Over To You.

How well do you know your people?

What really motivates them?

What's really important to them?

What is their self-interest?

Why do they make the choices that they make?

Do you have a common understanding of how to respond to changes in your environment?

Do leaders lead?

Or, do followers follow?

Who actually appoints the leader? Is it the leader, or is it the followers?

I could appoint myself the leader, announce that I am in charge and set off walking in one direction. What if nobody follows? Am I actually the leader or not?

I believe that there is a technical term for a leader without followers. They are known as 'a billy no-mates'. The advent of social media emphasises the principle that humans choose who they follow. Platforms such as twitter allow us all to follow, and importantly to unfollow, whoever we like. Is it possible for someone to decide to become a 'thought-leader'? Surely thought-leadership results when people decide to follow another person's thinking.

Animal Leaders

Interestingly, animal teams seem to have a very simple and highly effective method of choosing their leaders. Leaders in the animal kingdom are not self-selected, or chosen by an exclusive group. Very simply, the leader is the one that the other animals choose to follow. If a group of animals are searching for food, they will tend to follow the member of their team that has the most knowledge or experience about sources of food. For example, if there is one individual that knows how to navigate to a particularly good spot, the others will follow them. Bees are remarkably efficient at finding food, even over relatively large distances. So, how do a colony of bees ensure that they collectively make the most of the available food sources? Is it a case of every bee for himself? Do they randomly fly until they find food? If one bee finds a good source of food, are they the only ones to benefit? Or, is there a way of helping the whole colony find it? And, how do the colony know which sources of food are the best?

The bees answer is to send out foragers or scouts. These bees then communicate the quality of the food source they have found by way of a 'waggle dance'. The intensity of the dance relates directly to the quality of the food source (e.g. the nectar available in a patch of flowers). Therefore, the other foragers will follow those bees who display the strongest dances on a second visit. Some bees will therefore have more followers than others. They then set off to their chosen areas with their band of followers. It seems like a game of follow my leader. After several more scouting missions and displays of waggle dancing, the bees will have narrowed down to the best source of food. By default, they will have chosen to follow one of the bees to their source of food.

Importantly, the waggle dance is not a popularity contest for the bees. There is no benefit to each bee in becoming the leader. The only benefit comes if they all find the strongest food source. Therefore, there is no interest in the bee performing a great waggle dance in order to recruit followers. In animal teams, leadership tends to be allocated on a very functional basis.

How Do Humans Appoint Leaders?

What would happen if humans tried adopting the waggle dance approach? Would our dance just reflect the quality of the nectar that we found? Or, would we want to recruit followers to our team because we wanted to be 'the lead bee'? Would we feel more important because the other bees were following us? Is it possible that, as a society, we might also start to reward or recognise the lead bees more than the others? In doing so, would we create an incentive for bees to lead, rather than accurately reporting what they've found? And, if we did start to change the dynamic, would we actually end up destroying the very system that has served the bees?

Do we appoint leaders for a specific task, based on their

particular knowledge, experience or skills? Or do we choose leaders according to some other agendas? I suspect that humans confuse the very elegant and effective process that animals use because we introduce our ego. Our society tends to value leaders, recognise them and rewards them more highly. When we choose Prime Ministers and Presidents, we say that they have been "elected into power".

"If I'm the leader, maybe I'll get a bigger office and a car park space right outside the front door."

Therefore people tend to seek leadership positions because they provide us with status. Our hierarchical social system tends to be built upon leadership. Therefore privilege and power follows leadership. It's not a surprise that many people want to lead, but it does mean that the way we elect leaders differs markedly from animals. It is also possible that our leaders may not be those best suited to lead, but those with the greatest desire to lead.

Who Is Really Leading?

Whilst talking to animal teams researcher, Dr Dan Franks, I asked how you spot the leader in a flock of pigeons. "Is the leader the one at the front?", I asked. Dan told me that it's often not the one at the front, because it doesn't need to be. Pigeons, like most birds, don't have eyes that point forwards. Instead they have eyes on the sides of their heads which provide more of a 360 degree perspective. Therefore, the leader doesn't need to be at the front to be seen, they can be anywhere within the flock and often fly in the middle. So, how can you tell which bird is leading? The truth is very simple, and provided a 'light bulb moment' for me.

The leader is the one to whom the most attention is directed.

When the lead pigeon turns left, the flock follows.
This understanding can help us to identify the real leaders in the organisation. If I'm looking for the leaders, I don't tend to be interested in their job titles. Instead, I look for the amount of influence they have on those around them.

Former England football team manager, Sven Goran Eriksson, used the term "cultural architects" to describe those who influenced the organisation. These are the people who have the ability to shape the culture and are often the real leaders.

Why Should I Follow You?

Just as there needs to be a strong reason for individuals to belong to a team, there needs to be an equally compelling reason for individuals to follow a leader. Logically there must be a reason why they'd choose to follow one person over another. Followers can follow whoever they like. Followers have the freedom to ask why they should follow a particular leader. Of course our 'cats', with their tendency to think independently, are likely to ask that question with more intensity and may also require more robust answers. Those who think they would make good leaders themselves, are also likely to have a critical opinion about the leadership capabilities of others. When we understand this dynamic, we also understand some of the questions that govern people's decisions to follow.

"Why would I want to follow you?"

"How will it benefit me?"

"What can you, the leader, give me?"

If asked "Why should I follow you?", some leaders will give a very straight forward answer, "Because if you don't, I'll fire you". Whilst it might be an easy answer, how strong is it really? Is an answer like that really going to help a leader to galvanise their team of independent thinkers to deliver a great team performance? Is that the kind of answer that encourages a team to run through brick walls for their leader? What happens when the leader asks the team to go the extra mile and pull out all the stops?

Over To You.

Why should your team follow you?

How will it benefit them?

Why should your people follow the leaders in your organisation?

How does it serve them?

Why do you follow the people that you choose to follow?

Are your leaders those people who are best suited to leadership, or the ones with the greatest desire to lead?

Who are the real leaders in your organisation; the ones that have the greatest influence?

What I'm about to say is not new, or revolutionary. There is a temptation that you'll think, "Yeah, I know all that" and that you'll overlook the importance of it. Ridiculous as it sounds, most people know all of the 'secrets' to success. More often than not, those people who manage to achieve great success don't know anything more, or different, than the rest of us. What often separates the high achiever is simply that they put it into practice consistently.

At this point in the show, I would recommend asking a few questions as you read.

"How well do we actually do these things?"

"One a scale of 0-10 (with 10 being 'perfect'), how would we score?"

"When I look at my team, where do I see these things, and where don't I?"

"When do I see them, and when don't I?"

"What could we do to improve in these fundamentally important areas?"

Are We All On The Same Page... Really?

What is our reason for being? Are we all here for the same reason? Fundamentally, do we all have the same "why", or at least a complementary "why"?

I know this sounds elementary, but I see so many organisations that don't have this base understanding in place. Sometimes the organisation doesn't have a clear idea of why it exists, or fails to communicate it clearly. Therefore, it's tough for the people to know if their 'why' matches that of the organisation. Author Simon Sinek (2011) emphasises the importance of understanding and communicating the 'why' with clarity and consistency. Why does your team

35

exist? What's your purpose? Why does the world need you? Why are you important? Having a strong, compelling reason to exist is critically important if we want people to invest in the team.

When I ask this question to teams and organisations, I often get the headline answers. For example, if I ask a business leader they might say, "We're here to make a profit" or "To be number one in our sector" or "be the best". Unfortunately, on their own, these reasons are not very inspiring. In fact I find myself saying, "So, what?". In order to find the real 'why', we may have to go beyond the obvious and find the real value in what we do.

CASE STUDY

Winning Olympic Gold

I've spent a lot of time working in Olympic programmes and with Olympic athletes. In Olympic sports you might imagine that this compelling reason would be obvious. Surely this strong purpose is simple; to win an Olympic gold medal. However, on its own, that's not enough. Successful Olympic athletes often have a fairly extensive and dedicated support team. Even an individual athlete, such as a swimmer or a runner, will have a team that includes their coaches, sport scientists, physiotherapists, strength and conditioning specialist, nutritionist and sport psychologist. None of these people will be awarded an Olympic medal if the athlete is successful. So why should the members of the support team push themselves, and each other, to enable the athlete to win a medal? If we look at it in the cold light of day, the medal is just a metal disc on a ribbon. What's so special about that? Will it change the world?

In itself, the gold medal is not necessarily compelling. The strength of purpose comes through understanding what Olympic success means to everyone. What's the why? The meaning goes beyond acquiring a metal disc. Contributing to Olympic success gives everyone in the team a way of pushing themselves and exploring their potential, not just the athlete. Enabling the athlete to achieve their potential often requires the support team to do the same. In essence, my 'why' is the same as the athlete's. We're both aiming to realise our potential.

As well as having a strong reason, we also need to know that it is shared by the team members. Is this something that we all want to belong to and that we will all invest into? In the case of many animal teams, often the purpose is simply to ensure the survival of the species. However, the reason may not be as obvious for many human teams.

James Kerr (2013) became aware that the All Blacks' purpose was deeper than merely being the best rugby team on Earth or winning trophies. Although winning the World Cup sounds grand, you could ask why placing an oval ball over a white line on a field is important. The All Blacks understand that there is a deeper purpose. Their 'why' revolves around the desire to leave a legacy; to "leave the shirt in a better place" by honouring those who have come before, and those who will follow. The All Blacks also express this as their desire "to be a good ancestor". In life, there are many ways that we can be a good ancestor and leave our legacy. The All Blacks do it through rugby. It is this deeper purpose that is central to being an All Black.

What's The Real Agenda?

Humans find it difficult to function without some kind of meaning. We need to know why we do what we do. Why do I spend so much of my life working? What's it all for? Many people will say, "Because it pays the bills". They may work for the weekend, or work to provide for their family. Some people work to afford those things they've always desired; the car or the holiday perhaps. Others have career aspirations and find a sense of achievement in gaining promotion, rising through the ranks and attaining the recognition and rewards that follow.

It would be fair to ask, "What's the problem with that?". People will always have a diverse set of motives and agendas.

Sometimes these have little or no negative impact upon a team. However, there are times when the agendas of the individual compete with the team, and can detract from it. Let's work through a couple of examples.

Meet Brendan. Brendan is an ambitious young executive that has serious career aspirations. In his job application he stated that he was a driven individual that had his sights set on getting to the top. During the interview, he reinforced that he wanted to progress through the organisation and become a senior executive; he even hinted that he aspired to join the board of directors in time. Therefore, it's no surprise that Brendan's primary agenda is his own career progression. He wants to climb the corporate ladder as quickly as possible.

Knowing that is his agenda, it's also unsurprising that Brendan's decisions and behaviours reflect this. He looks to form alliances with those who he believes can enhance his position. He wants people to be impressed. Like everyone, Brendan faces choices. Should he present something accurately and factually, knowing that it could create a negative impression? Or could he 'dress' the information to create a better impression? If something has gone wrong, does he look for excuses or an opportunity to blame? Or does he take responsibility, admit fault and risk looking bad? What's most important to him? What's his agenda?

James Surowiecki (2004) states that "A 1962 study of young executives, for instance, found that the more anxious they were about moving up the job ladder, the less accurately they communicated problem-related information" (p. 205).

Here are a couple of other examples from client organisations that I work with.

CASE STUDY

Interviewing For A Manager

An executive coaching client of mine was interviewing for senior managers. One of his team had recommended an applicant with a strong CV and suggested that he be invited in for interview. During the interview, the candidate mentioned that he considered himself to be a popular manager and that he always strove to be liked by his team. Throughout the interview, he emphasised that he considered popularity to be of primary importance. These comments started alarm bells ringing in my client's mind. What will this manager do if they're faced with a choice between making an unpopular decision that is right, or a poor decision that will make them popular?

CASE STUDY

The Intellectual Gladiators

By their very nature, those people that become senior leaders tend to be experienced, knowledgeable and intelligent. It's also possible that they know this, and thrive on it. The result can be that the boardroom becomes an arena for intellectual jousting. It would be wrong of me to single out lawyers by way of an example or to suggest that all lawyers engage in this past-time (but in many cases it would be valid).

On a number of occasions I have watched the discussions unfold. There tends to be a point in time when the agenda changes from trying to answer the question (or solve the problem), to winning the argument or making a point. In fact, whilst in these environments I have even found people looking to intellectually spar with me. Whilst I'm not necessarily against sparring (as a challenge), I don't see it contributing to the discussion or helping us to answer the question. On one occasion I found myself saying to an Equity Partner, "I know you're keen to win, so can we agree that you win, and start focusing on finding a solution?".

Of course, humans make decisions and act out their agendas constantly. I've seen countless professional football managers who seem more interested in keeping their job than improving their team. Rather than choosing to take responsibility for a defeat or a poor performance, they often choose to blame poor refereeing decisions or 'bad luck'. Genuine improvement in performance requires us to take responsibility, learn and make changes. That tends to be the tougher route. It may also appear to compromise the manager's goal of keeping their job. Is it more important to perform well, or avoid looking bad?

What's Your Primary Agenda?

Promotion?

Maximising shareholder returns?

Exiting your business for the maximum capital value in three years?

Delivering exceptional service to customers?

You may look at these and say, "None of the above". Equally, you may see two or three things that resonate. The question in the sub-title (What Is Your Primary Agenda) recognises that there may be more than one motive. The word 'Primary' is critical. The question is, which agenda is most prominent?

What's Your Team's Agenda?

Your promotion?

Maximising shareholder returns / making shareholders richer?

Ensuring that you can exit the business with maximum capital value in three years?

Delivering great service to the customer?

Their own career progression?

Their own remuneration?

Something else?

Do you know what their agenda is? Does is align with yours? If not, it's likely that you'll find yourself in a tug-of-war. I also suspect that it will be pretty difficult to herd the cats.

So, how can we reduce the likelihood that personal agendas will compete with each other and the needs of the team?

Understand Our "Two Lengths Of The Pool".

I'd better start by explaining what the phrase 'Two Lengths of the Pool' means. Several years ago I worked with an Olympic swimmer. In total, Chris (the swimmer) and I worked together for around eight years. For the first three to four years we completely misunderstood his job. To begin with, we thought his job was to win... or to make the Great Britain team... or to secure sponsorship... or funding. We were wrong. None of those things were Chris' job. He was a 100 meter swimmer, and he swam in a 50 meter pool. His job, very simply, was to swim two lengths of the pool as fast as he could (Hartley, 2013).

Knowing your job in the simplest possible terms is extremely powerful. As an Olympic swimmer, Chris Cook had a team of specialists and coaches that worked with him. Each member of the team was an expert in their field. Each member brought thoughts, opinions and ideas to the table. Often there would be challenge, disagreement and some pretty frank exchanges of views. There was a real potential that things became personal, that people became defensive and that the discussions became competitive. However, none of these things did happen because we were all guided by a common question; will this help Chris to swim two lengths of the pool as quickly as possible? That's our agenda. We're not interested in who looks good, or who looks bad, or who 'wins' the argument. Our job here is to help this swimmer produce the fastest possible time in the pool.

If you'd like to know how to find your job in the simplest possible terms, read "Two Lengths of the Pool".

Inter-dependencies.

With a clear understanding of our "Two Lengths" and the deeper purpose behind it, we can help people to see why and how to contribute to the team. However, on a functional level, there is a potential that we could still inadvertently step on each other's toes. In our attempts to make sure that we deliver our objectives, we may inhibit someone else's ability to deliver theirs. Often we simply lack the awareness of what others need, because we're so focused on our own job. When we realise how we're dependent upon each other, we stand a much better chance of helping those around us to perform.

Do we inhibit each other's performance?

Do we allow each other to perform?

Do we actually enable each other to perform better?

Put simply, team members are not independent from each other, they are inter-dependent.

"I need you to do X, so that I can do Y, so that the team can deliver Z".

Rather than focusing on my priorities verses yours, we start by asking what the team needs and how we can both ensure that we deliver it. It often starts with simple questions like, "How do we make sure that we deliver our 'Two Lengths of the Pool'?" These conversations help us to understand that a task which is at the bottom of my priority list, might actually be at the top of the team's priority list. Although this task may not seem particularly important to me, neglecting it could have a knock on impact to the effectiveness of the whole team. To help identify some of these things, I recently asked a business team to complete some simple statements.

"At the moment I get frustrated when...."

"My life can be made more difficult if..."

"We would definitely step up a gear if we..."

"To do my job better, it would really help if..."

"If I could make a request of someone, I would ask..."

"I think I could help someone else by..."
"I can see an opportunity for us to be more effective if we..."

"We'd be a great team if we consistently..."

If we have a clear, strong and shared purpose, and we all understand the job simply and clearly, there is a very good chance that we'll actively do things that enable each other to perform better. In the absence of these things, we're likely to put our own priorities ahead of other peoples and focus on advancing our own agenda.

Over To You.

How strong is your "why" as an organisation?

What lies beyond the headlines?

What's your agenda?

What's the team's agenda?

How can you see these agendas displayed in people's decisions, choices and behaviours?

Are your agendas aligned?

Do you know your "Two Lengths of the Pool"?

Does the team know it?

Do your team members inhibit, allow or enable each other to perform?

So, how could you actually herd cats? To help answer that question, let's take a look at the feline cats to begin with. If we had a collection of cats in a room, how do we get them all into the same corner? Here are three options.

1. Impose a 24 hour fast so that the cats are hungry. In order to 'herd' the cats, simply place a bowl of food in the corner of the room. The hungry cats are likely to migrate towards the food.

2. Turn off the heating (or turn up the air conditioning) to cool the room. Then, place a nice warm electric blanked it the corner of the room. Cats tend to seek comfort, and are likely to make their way to the corner with the warm blanket.

3. Make an exit in one corner of the room and introduce a pack of hungry wolves into the opposite corner. It's a fair bet that the cats will all opt for the exit.

The principle is very simple. The solutions hinge around finding something that each of these independent thinkers will individually choose. In each case we're presenting an option that is in their best interests. In some cases, it's a "no brainer". These three examples provide the cats with something that they seek; satisfaction, nourishment, comfort and safety. Of course, it's not only cats that seek these things. Humans do too.

How Does It Apply To People?

Here are a few real world examples that might help to illustrate how these principles apply.

CASE STUDY

Professional Footballer

This particular player was six months from retiring as a

professional footballer. He had played over 400 matches in the English Premier League, and had been capped multiple times by his country. The club had noticed that his body fat levels had started to increase and they were keen to get him on a diet. Do you think he wanted to? Do you think he wanted to stop eating all the things he liked, and drinking what he wanted? Although his diet and drinking habits were far from ideal, he'd kept the same pattern throughout his career and been very successful. Why should he change now, just six months before retiring? Was he really interested in making his life more difficult in order to appease the club and lose a few millimetres of body fat? If you had simply asked him to go on a diet, his response would have been "**** off!" (...and that's the polite version).

I had a conversation with the player, and asked him what kind of life he saw for himself when he retired from the game. We talked about his health, and the future that he was likely to experience if his diet remained the same. Of course, when he retired, he wouldn't be training five days, and playing one or two competitive games, every week. He wasn't getting any younger, and had passed that dreaded "30 something" mark when the metabolism grinds to a halt. As a result, he was likely to put on significant weight if he kept eating and drinking as he'd done through his playing career. I asked him whether he thought he'd have great energy and health in five to ten years' time. Did he see a future in which he'd be playing football in the park with his kids? What did he want for himself?

It became obvious that he wanted to be healthy and active for many years to come. It was also fair to say that his current diet was unlikely to give him the future that he desired. I asked whether it made sense for him to tap into the resources at the club whilst he had free access to them. Why not use the fitness coach, the nutritionist and the physiologist, whilst you can? He agreed that it would be helpful and approached the sport science team for advice on how to lose some weight.

Importantly, the player chose to seek support for himself.

He wasn't doing it for the club, he was doing it because it benefitted him. And it happened to also be what the club wanted.

It's amazing what we can achieve when we actually align the interests of the individual with that of the team!

CASE STUDY

A New Fleet Sales Team

One of my corporate clients is a motor retail group. A few years ago they created a team dedicated to fleet sales. During the past few years this team had become really successful. Because they were specialists in fleet sales, they sold more vehicles with a better profit margin. At the same time, they were also able to give a better service to the customer and often managed to save the customer money. It seemed like a real win-win for everyone. So, the CEO decided to roll the model out across the group. In order to do this, all of the fleet sales executives within the dealerships needed to report to a new General Manager, who headed up the fleet sales team. In addition, some of their processes would change. Rather than preparing the cars within the dealership and then transporting them to the customer, these functions would be done centrally. The problem is that this took work from the dealerships' own service department and reduced their income.

The General Manager of the fleet sales department was given the job of getting all of the regional directors and dealership managers on board. However, the regional directors and dealership managers didn't fancy the idea. In their view, they were losing members of their team, losing 'power', losing control and losing income from their own dealerships. That doesn't sound like a great deal does it?

So, how does the Fleet Sales General Manager align everyone's' interests?

The answer was to start by finding the common ground. He asked, "What is our 'Two Lengths of the Pool', as a business?". Their job, collectively, was simply to sell as many vehicles as possible, profitably, and with great customer service. So, how could they do this? Was this change going to help them achieve their 'Two Lengths'? The answer was "yes". Once they'd agreed this, they then set about finding ways that were beneficial to all. They looked at potential barriers and found ways to overcome them. They knew that the new system created a collective benefit to the business as a whole. So, they found ways to ensure that when they adopted the new processes, and realised the benefits, those rewards would be shared by everyone. As a result, they found alignment.

There are some leaders, in the business world, that don't have the ability to simply 'three line whip' their teams. Managing Partners, for example, don't have employees. As their title suggests, they have partners. In a law firm, their role is often to run the business of the firm for the benefit of all of the partners. Therefore, many Managing Partners are elected by the other partners. The partners are not employees of each other, either. This dynamic presents an interesting challenge.

CASE STUDY

Creating A Team From Individuals

There have been many changes to the provision of legal services in the UK during recent years. Some market analysts have predicted that up to 80% of law firms will disappear. Gradually, smaller firms will either be acquired by bigger operators, or forced to become bigger by acquiring others. Therefore, the strategy for most is to become either predators or prey.

The Law Firm that I worked with had adopted an interesting, and rather unusual, strategy; to remain independent. To do this, they needed to become incredibly strong. Their proposition needed to be exceptionally good, and they needed to have considerable financial strength. If the firm could not do this, they knew they would be out-muscled by bigger firms and those growing through acquisition. Bigger firms have the potential to undercut prices because they have scale. In addition, the bigger firms are likely to gobble up market share and may even choose to 'buy market share' by slashing prices to gain new clients. Therefore the firm's challenge was simply to become excellent.

To do this, the Equity Partners (EPs) needed to become a formidable team. They needed to ensure that the standards throughout the firm were sky-high. This required them to hold each other to account for the performance of their teams. The team also needed to ensure that they each delivered their financial targets and tight credit control. Rather than focusing purely on their own "practices", all of the partners need to develop a wider view and focus on the success of the firm. Importantly, each of the partners knew that the traditional approach of working in silos would not serve them anymore. Therefore, there was a compelling reason to become a strong team.

Inevitably, doing all of this demands more of each partner. It meant having some tough conversations, asking difficult questions and coming up with the answers. Often the EPs were challenged to give and take criticism, which is something that didn't come naturally to many. It took them way outside of their comfort zone. The team members were asked to learn about areas of the business that they'd tended to ignore in the past. The new environment did not allow them to cruise.

Of course, there had to be a very good reason why the EPs would push themselves and each other beyond their cosy, familiar, comfort zones. Independence is something that they all value a great deal. They are united in their desire to be in control of their own destiny and create a firm that they can be proud of. It is something which they all want. Therefore, it is in all of their individual self-interests. This purpose provides the glue which galvanises the independent thinkers.

These examples show the importance of understanding the desires, agendas and aspirations of individuals, so that we can create genuine alignment. Remember, herding cats is simple when there is a reason for each individual to independently choose the same direction.

How do these principles apply to your own team?

Here are some questions and exercises that may help...

What's your greatest leadership challenge?

```



```

When you look at your team, who is playing in the team, and who plays for the team?

In the team...	For the team...

Who, within the team, presents you with the greatest challenge?

```



```

Where does competition exist between members of the team?

Where do you see a lack of alignment between the agenda of individual team members and that of the team?

What is their "why" and what is yours?

The Individual's "Why"	My "Why"	The Team's "Why"

How can you resolve these differences and find common ground?

Is your organisation's "why" strong enough and clear enough?

Is your "Two Lengths of the Pool" strong enough and clear enough?

We know why sheep flock, but why does your team need to operate as a team?

When you recruit people to the team, how do you know that there is a common agenda? Do you test this in any way? Could you test it?

What else can you do to apply these principles, and galvanise your team of independent thinkers?

You now have some practical principles, which can help you galvanise your team. I genuinely hope that you find them as valuable as I have. If you found this little book useful, you may also be interested in these....

Find out the eight common characteristics that differentiate world class performers.

Find out how to master your mental game and achieve your peak performance

Find out how to take on daunting or seemingly impossible challenges by managing the conversation between your ears.

Find clarity and simplicity by understanding your job in the simplest possible terms.

If you would like to take more steps towards becoming world class, why not **become a member of Be World Class**, by registering at www.be-world-class.com. When you register, you'll find footage from a host of live events, including "On... Herding Cats".

Membership of Be World Class is ideal for entrepreneurs, athletes, business executives, sports coaches & sport psychologists, business coaches, senior business leaders (CEOs and MDs), athletic directors and performance directors.

Members receive a vast array of tools and resources that focus on

- Maximising personal performance
- How to work towards becoming world class in your field
- How to take on 'impossible' challenges
- World class leadership
- How to develop world class teams

And

- How to build world class organisations

FREE BONUS MATERIAL

As a 'thank you' for reading this book, I'd like to offer you some exclusive free bonus materials. Simply go to www. be-world-class.com/bonus and register your details. You'll find a wealth of free information, including book chapters, interviews, podcasts, articles, webinars and videos.

If you have questions, or would like to join in discussions on world class performance, feel free to join the 'be world class' LinkedIn group and follow @worldclasssimon on Twitter.

Thank you.

| Bibliography and Useful Links.

BBC (2009) 'Dolphins Invent A New Strategy To Catch Fish'. Life. Available Online. http://www.bbc.co.uk/learningzone/clips/dolphins-invent-a-unique-hunting-strategy-to-catch-fish/14034.html

BBC (2011) 'Killer Whales Make Waves To Hunt Seals'. Frozen Planet. Available Online. http://www.bbc.co.uk/nature/15308790

Duke, R. (2008) 'Why students don't learn what we think we teach them?', Keynote Lecture. Cornell University. 17th April 2008.

Foster, E.A., Franks, D.W., Mazzi, S., Darden, S.K., Balcomb, K.C., Ford, J.K.B., Croft, D.P. (2012) 'Adaptive Prolonged Postreproductive Life Span in Killer Whales', Science, Vol. 337 no. 6100 p. 1313. 14 September 2012

Hartley, S.R. (2011) Peak Performance Every Time, London: Routledge.

Hartley, S.R. (2012) How To Shine; Insights into unlocking your potential from proven winners, Chichester: Capstone.

Hartley, S.R. (2013) Two Lengths of the Pool; Sometimes the simplest ideas have the greatest impact, Arkendale, UK: Be World Class.

Hartley, S.R. (2014) Could I Do That?, Chichester: Capstone.

Hartley, S.R. (2014) "On... Herding Cats", Be World Class TV. Available Online. www.be-world-class.com

Jackson, P. and Delehanty, H. (1995) Sacred Hoops: Spiritual Lessons of a Hardwood Warrior, NewYork: Hyperion.

Kerr, J. (2013) Legacy; 15 Lessons In Leadership, London: Constable Robinson.

Sinek, S. (2011) Start With Why, London: Portfolio Penguin.

Surowiecki, J (2004). The Wisdom Of Crowds; Why The Many Are Smarter Than The Few, New York: Random House.

Woodrow, F. and Acland, S. (2012) Elite!; The Secrets To Exceptional Leadership And Performance, London: Elliott & Thompson.

Simon Hartley is globally respected sport psychology consultant and performance coach. He helps athletes and business people throughout the world to get their mental game right. For almost 20 years, he has worked with gold medallists, world record holders, world champions, top five world ranked professional athletes and championship winning teams.

Simon has worked at the highest level of sport, including spells in Premiership football, Premiership rugby union, First Class County Cricket, Super League, golf, tennis, motor sport and with Great British Olympians.

Since 2005, Simon has also applied the principles of sport psychology to business, education, healthcare and the charity sector. This has included projects with some of the world's leading corporations and foremost executives. More recently, Simon has also become a respected author and international professional speaker.

17127797R00048

Printed in Poland
by Amazon Fulfillment
Poland Sp. z o.o., Wrocław